REASONS WHY BRITAIN SHOULD REMAIN IN THE EUROPEAN UNION & NOT BREXIT:

A COMPREHENSIVE GUIDE

BY

SUNSHINE SUZZII

© Copyright 2018 by Sunshine Suzzii
- All rights reserved.
ISBN-13: **978-1986544979**

Disclaimer
This document is for providing entertainment and tongue in cheek information in regards to the topic and issue covered. The publication is sold with the idea that the publisher is not required to render accounting, officially permitted, or otherwise, qualified services. If advice is necessary, legal or professional, a practiced individual in the profession should be ordered.

- From a Declaration of Principles which was accepted and approved equally by a Committee of the American Bar Association and a Committee of Publishers and Associations.

In no way is it legal to reproduce, duplicate, or transmit any part of this document in either electronic means or in printed format. Recording of this publication is strictly prohibited and any storage of this document is not allowed unless with written permission from the publisher. All rights reserved.

The information provided herein is stated to be truthful and consistent, in that any liability, in terms of inattention or otherwise, by any usage or abuse of any policies, processes, or directions contained within is the solitary and utter responsibility of the recipient reader. Under no circumstances will any legal responsibility or blame be held against the publisher for any reparation, damages, or monetary loss due to the information herein, either directly or indirectly.

Respective authors own all copyrights not held by the publisher.

The information herein is offered for informational purposes solely, and is universal as so. The presentation of the information is without contract or any type of guarantee assurance.

The trademarks that are used are without any consent, and the publication of the trademark is without permission or backing by the trademark owner. All trademarks if any or brands named within this book are for clarifying purposes only and are owned by the owners themselves, not affiliated with this document.

*Reasons Why Britain Should Remain in the European Union
& Not BREXIT*

Introduction

This is a book that might be read several times becoming more insightful and enhanced each time around. In my opinion, this is a must read for anyone wanting to leave the EU, and is essential reading for any young students out there.

As a comprehensive 'tongue-in-cheek' guide which is mostly blank, it contains 1,181 words; thorough imaginable debates taken from real, rational thinking behind the core reasons why Britain should not Brexit. Furthermore, if you were not convinced before reading this book, then it will certainly eliminate any doubt about whether Britain should Brexit or not.

The overarching message remains clear and should not be lost in translation, into other EU languages, so as to spread the important subliminal messages contained in this book about whether we should stay or go. No offense intended to either camps.

Reasons Why Britain Should Remain in the European Union & Not BREXIT

Introduction...........................6

Chapter 1 - Economics, Money Matters & Cheap Fast Food Chicken Shops 12

Chapter 2 - Foreign Policy & Decision-Making Mechanisms.......20

Chapter 3 - Democracy & the House of Commons...................................29

Chapter 4 – Education 39

Chapter 5 - Controlled Immigration, Identity Suppression: European Identity Forget Being Irish, Welsh, Scottish or British..........................50

Chapter 6 - No Skills Shortages, More Investments Means More Jobs 61

Chapter 7 - The National Health Service & the Welfare State 72

Chapter 8 - Safety, Security, No Crime with Law Enforcement Intelligence, Fingerprinting & DNA Information 83

Chapter 9 - Save Energy with Big Brother Smart Meters 84

Chapter 10 - Forever Duty Bound by NATO Treaty When a Member State is under Attack.................................95

Chapter 11 – 1950s Common Market: No War between EU Folk.............106

Chapter 12 - Caring is Sharing Authority & Sovereignty: A Meaty Treaty Served with Brussels..........115

Chapter 13 - International Trade Not Free Trade: Britain, You'll Never Walk Alone....................................124

Chapter 14 - Belgian Chocolates, Danish Bacon, French / Italian Wine & Cheap German Cars, All Tariffs Free..132

Chapter 15 – No Visas: Easier to Backpack or Play Footie around Europe..144

Chapter 16 – Housing Issues: Slim Chance of Millennials Buying First Home, No Chance after BREXIT ..155

Chapter 17 - No More Bendy Bananas...166

Chapter 18 - Less Energy Wastage & Lesser Global Warming, Dimmed

Lights & Weaker Household Appliances 172

Chapter 19 - European Laws Made by Elected Bureaucrats in Brussels ...181

Chapter 20 - Britain the Wealthier State: Supports the EU National Economy Costs & Funds EU Projects 188

Chapter 21 - The European Economic Community 1973, European Union Today, One World Government Order by Next Week 200

Chapter 22 – No Need to Ever Reclaim Control over Our Own Frontiers Again 208

Chapter 23 - British Film Industry & Netflix will Flourish More Than Before 215

Chapter 24 Britain Earns Respect from America, Japan & China 225

Chapter 25 - How Democratically Accountable is the European Union? 231

Chapter 26 - Little Englanders Living in Spain Make UK Visits to Family, the NHS & Pick up Their Postal Mail 238

Bibliography 243

About the Author..........................244

Reasons Why Britain Should Remain in the European Union & Not BREXIT

Chapter 1 - Economics, Money Matters & Cheap Fast Food Chicken Shops

Reasons Why Britain Should Remain in the European Union & Not BREXIT

Reasons Why Britain Should Remain in the European Union & Not BREXIT

Reasons Why Britain Should Remain in the European Union & Not BREXIT

Reasons Why Britain Should Remain in the European Union & Not BREXIT

Reasons Why Britain Should Remain in the European Union & Not BREXIT

Reasons Why Britain Should Remain in the European Union & Not BREXIT

*Reasons Why Britain Should Remain in the European Union
& Not BREXIT*

Chapter 2 - Foreign Policy & Decision-Making Mechanisms

*Reasons Why Britain Should Remain in the European Union
& Not BREXIT*

Reasons Why Britain Should Remain in the European Union & Not BREXIT

Reasons Why Britain Should Remain in the European Union & Not BREXIT

Reasons Why Britain Should Remain in the European Union & Not BREXIT

Reasons Why Britain Should Remain in the European Union & Not BREXIT

*Reasons Why Britain Should Remain in the European Union
& Not BREXIT*

Reasons Why Britain Should Remain in the European Union & Not BREXIT

Reasons Why Britain Should Remain in the European Union & Not BREXIT

Chapter 3 - Democracy & the House of Commons

*Reasons Why Britain Should Remain in the European Union
& Not BREXIT*

Reasons Why Britain Should Remain in the European Union & Not BREXIT

Reasons Why Britain Should Remain in the European Union & Not BREXIT

Reasons Why Britain Should Remain in the European Union & Not BREXIT

Reasons Why Britain Should Remain in the European Union & Not BREXIT

Reasons Why Britain Should Remain in the European Union & Not BREXIT

Reasons Why Britain Should Remain in the European Union & Not BREXIT

Reasons Why Britain Should Remain in the European Union & Not BREXIT

Reasons Why Britain Should Remain in the European Union & Not BREXIT

Chapter 4 – Education

*Reasons Why Britain Should Remain in the European Union
& Not BREXIT*

Reasons Why Britain Should Remain in the European Union & Not BREXIT

Reasons Why Britain Should Remain in the European Union & Not BREXIT

*Reasons Why Britain Should Remain in the European Union
& Not BREXIT*

Reasons Why Britain Should Remain in the European Union & Not BREXIT

*Reasons Why Britain Should Remain in the European Union
& Not BREXIT*

*Reasons Why Britain Should Remain in the European Union
& Not BREXIT*

Reasons Why Britain Should Remain in the European Union & Not BREXIT

Reasons Why Britain Should Remain in the European Union & Not BREXIT

Reasons Why Britain Should Remain in the European Union & Not BREXIT

Chapter 5 - Controlled Immigration, Identity Suppression: European Identity Forget Being Irish, Welsh, Scottish or British

Reasons Why Britain Should Remain in the European Union & Not BREXIT

*Reasons Why Britain Should Remain in the European Union
& Not BREXIT*

Reasons Why Britain Should Remain in the European Union & Not BREXIT

*Reasons Why Britain Should Remain in the European Union
& Not BREXIT*

Reasons Why Britain Should Remain in the European Union & Not BREXIT

*Reasons Why Britain Should Remain in the European Union
& Not BREXIT*

Reasons Why Britain Should Remain in the European Union & Not BREXIT

Reasons Why Britain Should Remain in the European Union & Not BREXIT

*Reasons Why Britain Should Remain in the European Union
& Not BREXIT*

Reasons Why Britain Should Remain in the European Union & Not BREXIT

Chapter 6 - No Skills Shortages, More Investments Means More Jobs

Reasons Why Britain Should Remain in the European Union & Not BREXIT

Reasons Why Britain Should Remain in the European Union & Not BREXIT

Reasons Why Britain Should Remain in the European Union & Not BREXIT

*Reasons Why Britain Should Remain in the European Union
& Not BREXIT*

Reasons Why Britain Should Remain in the European Union & Not BREXIT

Reasons Why Britain Should Remain in the European Union & Not BREXIT

Reasons Why Britain Should Remain in the European Union & Not BREXIT

Reasons Why Britain Should Remain in the European Union & Not BREXIT

*Reasons Why Britain Should Remain in the European Union
& Not BREXIT*

*Reasons Why Britain Should Remain in the European Union
& Not BREXIT*

Chapter 7 - The National Health Service & the Welfare State

*Reasons Why Britain Should Remain in the European Union
& Not BREXIT*

Reasons Why Britain Should Remain in the European Union & Not BREXIT

Reasons Why Britain Should Remain in the European Union & Not BREXIT

Reasons Why Britain Should Remain in the European Union & Not BREXIT

Reasons Why Britain Should Remain in the European Union & Not BREXIT

*Reasons Why Britain Should Remain in the European Union
& Not BREXIT*

*Reasons Why Britain Should Remain in the European Union
& Not BREXIT*

*Reasons Why Britain Should Remain in the European Union
& Not BREXIT*

Reasons Why Britain Should Remain in the European Union & Not BREXIT

Reasons Why Britain Should Remain in the European Union & Not BREXIT

Chapter 8 - Safety, Security, No Crime with Law Enforcement Intelligence, Fingerprinting & DNA Information

Reasons Why Britain Should Remain in the European Union & Not BREXIT

Chapter 9 - Save Energy with Big Brother Smart Meters

Reasons Why Britain Should Remain in the European Union & Not BREXIT

Reasons Why Britain Should Remain in the European Union & Not BREXIT

Reasons Why Britain Should Remain in the European Union & Not BREXIT

Reasons Why Britain Should Remain in the European Union & Not BREXIT

Reasons Why Britain Should Remain in the European Union & Not BREXIT

Reasons Why Britain Should Remain in the European Union & Not BREXIT

Reasons Why Britain Should Remain in the European Union & Not BREXIT

Reasons Why Britain Should Remain in the European Union & Not BREXIT

Reasons Why Britain Should Remain in the European Union & Not BREXIT

Reasons Why Britain Should Remain in the European Union & Not BREXIT

Chapter 10 - Forever Duty Bound by NATO Treaty When a Member State is under Attack

Reasons Why Britain Should Remain in the European Union & Not BREXIT

*Reasons Why Britain Should Remain in the European Union
& Not BREXIT*

*Reasons Why Britain Should Remain in the European Union
& Not BREXIT*

Reasons Why Britain Should Remain in the European Union & Not BREXIT

Reasons Why Britain Should Remain in the European Union & Not BREXIT

Reasons Why Britain Should Remain in the European Union & Not BREXIT

Reasons Why Britain Should Remain in the European Union & Not BREXIT

Reasons Why Britain Should Remain in the European Union
& Not BREXIT

Reasons Why Britain Should Remain in the European Union & Not BREXIT

Reasons Why Britain Should Remain in the European Union & Not BREXIT

Chapter 11 – 1950s Common Market: No War between EU Folk

Reasons Why Britain Should Remain in the European Union & Not BREXIT

Reasons Why Britain Should Remain in the European Union & Not BREXIT

*Reasons Why Britain Should Remain in the European Union
& Not BREXIT*

Reasons Why Britain Should Remain in the European Union & Not BREXIT

Reasons Why Britain Should Remain in the European Union & Not BREXIT

Reasons Why Britain Should Remain in the European Union & Not BREXIT

Reasons Why Britain Should Remain in the European Union & Not BREXIT

Reasons Why Britain Should Remain in the European Union & Not BREXIT

Chapter 12 - Caring is Sharing Authority & Sovereignty: A Meaty Treaty Served with Brussels

*Reasons Why Britain Should Remain in the European Union
& Not BREXIT*

Reasons Why Britain Should Remain in the European Union & Not BREXIT

*Reasons Why Britain Should Remain in the European Union
& Not BREXIT*

Reasons Why Britain Should Remain in the European Union & Not BREXIT

Reasons Why Britain Should Remain in the European Union & Not BREXIT

*Reasons Why Britain Should Remain in the European Union
& Not BREXIT*

Reasons Why Britain Should Remain in the European Union & Not BREXIT

Reasons Why Britain Should Remain in the European Union & Not BREXIT

Chapter 13 - International Trade Not Free Trade: Britain, You'll Never Walk Alone

Reasons Why Britain Should Remain in the European Union & Not BREXIT

Reasons Why Britain Should Remain in the European Union & Not BREXIT

Reasons Why Britain Should Remain in the European Union & Not BREXIT

Reasons Why Britain Should Remain in the European Union & Not BREXIT

Reasons Why Britain Should Remain in the European Union & Not BREXIT

Reasons Why Britain Should Remain in the European Union & Not BREXIT

Reasons Why Britain Should Remain in the European Union & Not BREXIT

Chapter 14 - Belgian Chocolates, Danish Bacon, French / Italian Wine & Cheap German Cars, All Tariffs Free

*Reasons Why Britain Should Remain in the European Union
& Not BREXIT*

Reasons Why Britain Should Remain in the European Union & Not BREXIT

Reasons Why Britain Should Remain in the European Union & Not BREXIT

Reasons Why Britain Should Remain in the European Union & Not BREXIT

Reasons Why Britain Should Remain in the European Union & Not BREXIT

Reasons Why Britain Should Remain in the European Union & Not BREXIT

Reasons Why Britain Should Remain in the European Union & Not BREXIT

Reasons Why Britain Should Remain in the European Union & Not BREXIT

Reasons Why Britain Should Remain in the European Union & Not BREXIT

Reasons Why Britain Should Remain in the European Union & Not BREXIT

Reasons Why Britain Should Remain in the European Union & Not BREXIT

Chapter 15 – No Visas: Easier to Backpack or Play Footie around Europe

Reasons Why Britain Should Remain in the European Union
& Not BREXIT

Reasons Why Britain Should Remain in the European Union & Not BREXIT

*Reasons Why Britain Should Remain in the European Union
& Not BREXIT*

Reasons Why Britain Should Remain in the European Union & Not BREXIT

Reasons Why Britain Should Remain in the European Union & Not BREXIT

Reasons Why Britain Should Remain in the European Union & Not BREXIT

*Reasons Why Britain Should Remain in the European Union
& Not BREXIT*

Reasons Why Britain Should Remain in the European Union & Not BREXIT

*Reasons Why Britain Should Remain in the European Union
& Not BREXIT*

Reasons Why Britain Should Remain in the European Union & Not BREXIT

Chapter 16 – Housing Issues: Slim Chance of Millennials Buying First Home, No Chance after BREXIT

Reasons Why Britain Should Remain in the European Union & Not BREXIT

Reasons Why Britain Should Remain in the European Union & Not BREXIT

Reasons Why Britain Should Remain in the European Union & Not BREXIT

Reasons Why Britain Should Remain in the European Union & Not BREXIT

Reasons Why Britain Should Remain in the European Union & Not BREXIT

Reasons Why Britain Should Remain in the European Union & Not BREXIT

Reasons Why Britain Should Remain in the European Union & Not BREXIT

Reasons Why Britain Should Remain in the European Union & Not BREXIT

Reasons Why Britain Should Remain in the European Union & Not BREXIT

Reasons Why Britain Should Remain in the European Union & Not BREXIT

Reasons Why Britain Should Remain in the European Union & Not BREXIT

Chapter 17 - No More Bendy Bananas

*Reasons Why Britain Should Remain in the European Union
& Not BREXIT*

Reasons Why Britain Should Remain in the European Union & Not BREXIT

*Reasons Why Britain Should Remain in the European Union
& Not BREXIT*

*Reasons Why Britain Should Remain in the European Union
& Not BREXIT*

Reasons Why Britain Should Remain in the European Union & Not BREXIT

Reasons Why Britain Should Remain in the European Union & Not BREXIT

Chapter 18 - Less Energy Wastage & Lesser Global Warming, Dimmed Lights & Weaker Household Appliances

*Reasons Why Britain Should Remain in the European Union
& Not BREXIT*

Reasons Why Britain Should Remain in the European Union & Not BREXIT

Reasons Why Britain Should Remain in the European Union & Not BREXIT

*Reasons Why Britain Should Remain in the European Union
& Not BREXIT*

Reasons Why Britain Should Remain in the European Union & Not BREXIT

Reasons Why Britain Should Remain in the European Union & Not BREXIT

Reasons Why Britain Should Remain in the European Union & Not BREXIT

Reasons Why Britain Should Remain in the European Union & Not BREXIT

Chapter 19 - European Laws Made by Elected Bureaucrats in Brussels

*Reasons Why Britain Should Remain in the European Union
& Not BREXIT*

Reasons Why Britain Should Remain in the European Union & Not BREXIT

Reasons Why Britain Should Remain in the European Union & Not BREXIT

Reasons Why Britain Should Remain in the European Union & Not BREXIT

Reasons Why Britain Should Remain in the European Union & Not BREXIT

Reasons Why Britain Should Remain in the European Union
& Not BREXIT

Chapter 20 - Britain the Wealthier State: Supports the EU National Economy Costs & Funds EU Projects

Reasons Why Britain Should Remain in the European Union & Not BREXIT

Reasons Why Britain Should Remain in the European Union & Not BREXIT

*Reasons Why Britain Should Remain in the European Union
& Not BREXIT*

Reasons Why Britain Should Remain in the European Union & Not BREXIT

*Reasons Why Britain Should Remain in the European Union
& Not BREXIT*

*Reasons Why Britain Should Remain in the European Union
& Not BREXIT*

Reasons Why Britain Should Remain in the European Union & Not BREXIT

*Reasons Why Britain Should Remain in the European Union
& Not BREXIT*

*Reasons Why Britain Should Remain in the European Union
& Not BREXIT*

Reasons Why Britain Should Remain in the European Union & Not BREXIT

*Reasons Why Britain Should Remain in the European Union
& Not BREXIT*

Chapter 21 - The European Economic Community 1973, European Union Today, One World Government Order by Next Week

Reasons Why Britain Should Remain in the European Union & Not BREXIT

Reasons Why Britain Should Remain in the European Union & Not BREXIT

Reasons Why Britain Should Remain in the European Union & Not BREXIT

Reasons Why Britain Should Remain in the European Union & Not BREXIT

Reasons Why Britain Should Remain in the European Union & Not BREXIT

Reasons Why Britain Should Remain in the European Union & Not BREXIT

*Reasons Why Britain Should Remain in the European Union
& Not BREXIT*

Chapter 22 – No Need to Ever Reclaim Control over Our Own Frontiers Again

*Reasons Why Britain Should Remain in the European Union
& Not BREXIT*

Reasons Why Britain Should Remain in the European Union & Not BREXIT

*Reasons Why Britain Should Remain in the European Union
& Not BREXIT*

*Reasons Why Britain Should Remain in the European Union
& Not BREXIT*

Reasons Why Britain Should Remain in the European Union & Not BREXIT

Reasons Why Britain Should Remain in the European Union & Not BREXIT

Chapter 23 - British Film Industry & Netflix will Flourish More Than Before

Reasons Why Britain Should Remain in the European Union & Not BREXIT

*Reasons Why Britain Should Remain in the European Union
& Not BREXIT*

Reasons Why Britain Should Remain in the European Union & Not BREXIT

Reasons Why Britain Should Remain in the European Union & Not BREXIT

Reasons Why Britain Should Remain in the European Union & Not BREXIT

*Reasons Why Britain Should Remain in the European Union
& Not BREXIT*

Reasons Why Britain Should Remain in the European Union & Not BREXIT

*Reasons Why Britain Should Remain in the European Union
& Not BREXIT*

*Reasons Why Britain Should Remain in the European Union
& Not BREXIT*

Chapter 24 Britain Earns Respect from America, Japan & China

Reasons Why Britain Should Remain in the European Union & Not BREXIT

Reasons Why Britain Should Remain in the European Union & Not BREXIT

Reasons Why Britain Should Remain in the European Union & Not BREXIT

*Reasons Why Britain Should Remain in the European Union
& Not BREXIT*

*Reasons Why Britain Should Remain in the European Union
& Not BREXIT*

Chapter 25 - How Democratically Accountable is the European Union?

*Reasons Why Britain Should Remain in the European Union
& Not BREXIT*

Reasons Why Britain Should Remain in the European Union & Not BREXIT

Reasons Why Britain Should Remain in the European Union & Not BREXIT

Reasons Why Britain Should Remain in the European Union & Not BREXIT

*Reasons Why Britain Should Remain in the European Union
& Not BREXIT*

Reasons Why Britain Should Remain in the European Union & Not BREXIT

Chapter 26 - Little Englanders Living in Spain Make UK Visits to Family, the NHS & Pick up Their Postal Mail

Reasons Why Britain Should Remain in the European Union & Not BREXIT

*Reasons Why Britain Should Remain in the European Union
& Not BREXIT*

*Reasons Why Britain Should Remain in the European Union
& Not BREXIT*

Reasons Why Britain Should Remain in the European Union & Not BREXIT

Bibliography

About the Author

Sunshine Suzzii is a philanthropist and an avid dog and cat lover, she enjoys writing comedy.

*Reasons Why Britain Should Remain in the European Union
& Not BREXIT*

www.ingramcontent.com/pod-product-compliance
Lightning Source LLC
Chambersburg PA
CBHW031615210526
45464CB00004B/1595